# Contents

KU-327-113

Move!. . . . . . . . . . . . . . 4

School . . . . . . . . . . . . 6

Practice. . . . . . . . . . . 10

Outdoors . . . . . . . . . . 16

Glossary . . . . . . . . . . 22
Find out more . . . . . . . 23
Comprehension
  questions. . . . . . . . . . 24
Index. . . . . . . . . . . .24

# Move!

I want to stay healthy!

I move a lot each day.

My body stays active.

Little Pebble™

Healthy Me

# I STAY ACTIVE

by Martha E. H. Rustad

Raintree is an imprint of Capstone Global Library Limited, a company incorporated in England and Wales having its registered office at 264 Banbury Road, Oxford, OX2 7DY – Registered company number: 6695582

www.raintree.co.uk
myorders@raintree.co.uk

Edited by Shelly Lyons
Designed by Juliette Peters
Picture research by Jo Miller
Production by Tori Abraham

ISBN 978 1 4747 3484 4 (hardback)
20 19 18 17 16
10 9 8 7 6 5 4 3 2 1

ISBN 978 1 4747 3488 2 (paperback)
21 20 19 18 17
10 9 8 7 6 5 4 3 2 1

British Library Cataloguing in Publication Data
A full catalogue record for this book is available from the Briti

Acknowledgements
Images by Capstone Studio: Karon Dubke
Photo Styling: Sarah Schuette and Marcy Morin

Every effort has been made to contact copyright holders of material reproduced in this book. Any omissions will be rectified in subsequent printings if notice is given to the publisher.

All the Internet addresses (URLs) given in this book were valid at the time of going to press. However, due to the dynamic nature of the Internet, some addresses may have changed, or sites may have changed or ceased to exist since publication. While the author and publisher regret any inconvenience this may cause readers, no responsibility for any such changes can be accepted by either the author or the publisher.

Printed and bound in India.

# School

I go outside at playtime.

I hang from the monkey bars.

My muscles stay strong.

My class does P.E.
We play tag.
Running keeps
my heart healthy.

# Practice

I go to football practice.

We play a game.

I save a goal!

My sister is a gymnast.

I cheer for her.

She does a flip!

My brother swims.

He goes to a swimming club.

He swims fast.

# Outdoors

In winter we go sledging.

We climb up a steep hill.

I sledge down.

Whee!

In summer we go hiking.

We find a path and walk.

We stop to drink water.

I play at the park.

I keep my body moving.

Staying active means

a healthy me!

I play at the park.

I keep my body moving.

Staying active means

a healthy me!

# Glossary

**active**   being busy and moving around

**heart**   a muscle that moves blood in your body

**hike**   to go for a long walk outside

**muscle**   a band of body tissues that help the body move

**playtime**   a break during school; students often go outside at playtime.

# Find out more

## Books

*Exercising* (Take Care of Yourself!), Sian Smith (Raintree, 2013)

*Keeping Fit* (Let's Read and Talk About), Honor Head (Franklin Watts, 2014)

*Exercise* (Being Healthy, Feeling Great), Robyn Hardyman (Wayland, 2012)

## Websites

kidshealth.org/en/kids/stay-healthy/
Tips on keeping fit and having fun.

www.bbc.co.uk/guides/zxvkd2p
A video shows you how to stay healthy.

www.childrensuniversity.manchester.ac.uk/interactives/science/exercise/
Find out why exercise is so important.

# Comprehension questions

1. On page 18, what do they stop to do?

2. Why is it important to keep your heart healthy?

3. What are muscles? Why are your muscles important?

# Index

drinking water  18
gymnastics  12
hearts  8
hiking  18
muscles  6
P.E.  8

playing  6, 8, 20
playtime  6
practice  10
running  8
sledging  16
swimming  14